Cloud 9 REVISION FOR MARY SHELLEY'S *FRANKENSTEIN* - Study guide (All chapters, page-by-page analysis)

CW00866701

by Joe Broadfoot MA

ISBN-13:
978-1979007917

ISBN-10:
1979007918

9-1 GCSE REVISION NOTES – FRANKENSTEIN

CONTENTS

Introduction 3
Best essay practice 4
Essay planning 5
New specification 8
Context 11
Letter One 17
Letter Two 18
Letter Three 19
Letter Four 20
Chapter One 23
Chapter Two 24
Chapter Three 26
Chapter Four 28
Character Five 30
Chapter Six 33
Chapter Seven 35
Chapter Eight 37
Chapter Nine 39
Chapter Ten 41
Chapter Eleven 42
Chapter Twelve 44
Chapter Thirteen 46
Chapter Fourteen 47
Chapter Fifteen 48
Chapter Sixteen 49
Chapter Seventeen 51
Chapter Eighteen 52
Chapter Nineteen 54
Chapter Twenty 56
Chapter Twenty-One 58
Chapter Twenty-Two 60
Chapter Twenty-Three 61
Chapter Twenty-Four 62
Glossary 66

Brief Introduction

This book is aimed at GCSE students of English Literature who are studying Mary Shelley's *Frankenstein*. The focus is on what examiners are looking for, especially since the changes to the curriculum in 2015, and here you will find each chapter covered in detail. I hope this will help you and be a valuable tool in your studies and revision.

Criteria for high marks

Make sure you use appropriate critical language (see glossary of literary terms at the back). You need your argument to be fluent, well-structured and coherent. Stay focused!

Analyse and explore the use of form, structure and the language. Explore how these aspects affect the meaning. Make connections between texts and look at different interpretations. Explore their strengths and weaknesses. Don't forget to use supporting references to strengthen your argument.

Analyse and explore the context.

Best essay practice

9-1 GCSE REVISION NOTES – FRANKENSTEIN

There are so many way to write an essay. Many schools use **PEE** for paragraphs: point/evidence/explain. Others use **PETER**: point/evidence/technique/explain/reader; **PEEL**: point, example, explain, link; **PEEE**: point/evidence/explain/explore. Whichever method you use, make sure you mention the **writer's effects**. This generally is what most students forget to add. You must think of what the writer is trying to achieve by using a particular technique and what is actually achieved. Do not just spot techniques and note them. You may get some credit for using appropriate technology, but unless you can comment on the effect created on the reader and/or the writer's intention, you will miss out on most of the marks available.

Essay planning

In order to write a good essay it is necessary to plan. In fact, it is best to quite formulaic in an exam situation, as you won't have much time to get started. Therefore I will ask you to learn the following acronym: **DATMC (Definition, Application, Terminology, Main, Conclusion**. Some schools call it: **GSLMC (General, Specific, Link, Main, Conclusion)**, but it amounts to the same thing. The first three letters concern the introduction. (Of course, the alternative is to leave some blank lines and write your introduction after you have completed the main body of your essay, but it is probably not advisable for most students).

Let us first look at the following exam question, which is on poetry (of course, the same essay-planning principles apply to essays on novels and plays as well).

QUESTION: Explore how the poet conveys **feelings** in the poem.

STEP ONE: Identify the **keyword** in the question. (I have already done this, by highlighting it in **bold**). If you are following GSLMC, you now need to make a **general statement** about what feelings are. Alternatively, if you're following DATMC, simply **define** 'feelings'. For example, 'Feelings are emotion states or reactions or vague, irrationals ideas and beliefs'.

STEP TWO: If you are following GSLMC, you now need to make a **specific statement** linking feelings (or whatever else you've defined) to how they appear in the poem. Alternatively, if you're following DATMC, simply define which 'feelings' **apply** in this poem. For example, 'The feelings love, fear and guilt appear in this poem, and are expressed by the speaker in varying degrees.'

STEP THREE: If you are following GSLMC, you now need to make a **link statement** identifying the methods used to convey the feelings (or whatever else you've defined) in the poem. Alternatively, if you're following DATMC, simply define which **techniques** are used to convey 'feelings' in this poem. For example, 'The poet primarily uses alliteration to emphasise his heightened emotional state, while hyperbole and enjambment also help to convey the sense that the speaker is descending into a state of madness.

STEP FOUR: Whether you are following GSLMC or DATMC, the next stage is more or less the same. The main part of the essay involves writing around **six paragraphs**, using whichever variation of PEEE you prefer. In my example, I will use **Point, Evidence, Exploration, Effect** on the listener. To make your essay even stronger, try to use your quotations chronologically. It will be easier for the examiner to follow, which means you are more likely to achieve a higher grade. To be more specific, I recommend that you take and analyse two quotations from the beginning of the poem, two from the middle, and two at the end.

STEP FIVE: Using Carol Ann Duffy's poem, 'Stealing', here's an example of how you could word one of your six paragraphs: **(POINT)** 'Near the beginning of the poem, the speaker's determination is expressed.' **(EVIDENCE)** 'This is achieved through the words: 'Better off dead than giving in'. **(EXPLORATION)**. The use of 'dead' emphasizes how far the speaker is prepared to go in pursuit of what he wants, although there is a sense that he is exaggerating (hyperbole). **(EFFECT)** The listener senses that the speaker may be immature given how prone he is to exaggerate his own bravery.

STEP SIX: After writing five or more paragraphs like the one above, it will be time to write a **conclusion**. In order to do that, it is necessary to sum up your previous points and evaluate them. This is not the time to introduce additional quotations. Here is an example of what I mean: 'To conclude, the poet clearly conveys the speaker's anger. Although the listener will be reluctant to completely sympathise with a thief, there is a sense that the speaker is suffering mentally, which makes him an interesting and partially a sympathetic character. By using a dramatic monologue form, the poet effectively conveys the speaker's mental anguish, which makes it easier to more deeply understand what first appears to be inexplicable acts of violence.

Other tips

Make your studies active!
Don't just sit there reading! Never forget to annotate, annotate and annotate!

All page references refer to the 2003 edition of *Frankenstein* published by Penguin Books (ISBN-13: 978-0-141-43947-1).

Frankenstein
AQA (New specification starting in 2015)

If you're studying for an AQA qualification in English Literature, there's a good chance your teachers will choose this text to study. There are good reasons for that: it's moralistic and familiar to students. The text encourages us to think about right and wrong.

However, one of the difficulties is the language. That can't be helped, bearing in mind that part A of the exam paper involves answering questions on Shakespeare, whereas part B is all about the 19th-century novel.

To further complicate things, the education system is in a state of flux: that means we have to be ready for constant change. Of course, everyone had got used to grades A,B and C meaning a pass. It was simple, it was straightforward and nearly everyone understood it. Please be prepared that from this day henceforward, the top grade will now be known as 9. A grade 4 will be a pass, and anything below that will be found and anything above it will be a pass. Hopefully, that's not too confusing for anyone!

Now onto the exam itself. As I said, paper 1 consists of Shakespeare and the 19th-century novel. It is a written closed book exam (in other words you are not allowed to have the texts with you), which lasts one hour 45 minutes. You can score 64 marks, which amounts to 40% of your GCSE grade. The other 60% is gained from paper 2, which is all about modern texts, poetry and unseen poetry. But enough about paper 2, as our concern here is paper 1 and more specifically section B: the 19th-century novel.

In section B, students will be expected to write in detail about an extract from the novel they have studied in class and then write about the novel as a whole. Just for the record, the other choices of novel are the following: *The Strange Case of Dr Jekyll and Mr Hyde* by Robert Louis Stevenson, *Great Expectations* by Charles Dickens, *Jane Eyre* by Charlotte Brontë, *A Christmas Carol* by Charles Dickens, *Pride and Prejudice* by Jane Austin, and *The Sign of Four* by Sir Arthur Conan Doyle. Of course, all the above novels are well worth a read, but for our purposes we will simply concentrate on *Frankenstein* by Mary Shelley.

Another important thing to consider is the fact that for section B of paper 1, you will not be assessed on assessment objective 4 (AO4), which involves spelling, punctuation, grammar and vocabulary. This will be assessed on section A of paper 1, which is about Shakespeare, and it will be worth 2.5% of your overall GCSE grade. In terms of raw marks, it is worth 4 out of 64. So for once, we need not concern ourselves with what is affectionately known as 'SPAG' too much.

However, it is necessary to use the correct literary terminology wherever possible to make sure we maximise our marks on assessment objective2 (AO2). AO2 tests how well we can analyse language form and structure. Additionally, we are expected to state the effect the writer tried to create and how it impacts on the reader. This brings me onto assessment objective 1 (AO1), which involves you writing a personal response to the text. It is important that you use quotations to backup your points of view. Like AO2, AO1 is worth 15% of your GCSE on Paper 1.

Assessment objective 3 (AO3) is worth half of that, but nevertheless it is important to comment on context to make sure you get as much of the 7.5% up for grabs as you can.

So just to make myself clear, there are 30 marks available in section B for your answer on the 19th-century novel. Breaking it down even further, you will get 12 marks maximum the backing up your personal opinion with quotations, an additional 12 marks for analysing the writer's choice of words for effect (not forgetting to use appropriate terminology - more on that see the glossary at the back of this book), and six marks for discussing context.

To make sure that you meet AQA's learning objectives and get a high mark, make sure you go into the exam knowing something about the following:

- the plot
- the characters
- the theme
- selected quotations/details
- exam skills

CONTEXT

The offspring of two famous radicals, the atheist William

Godwin (1756-1836) and the early feminist Mary Wollstonecraft (1759-97), Mary Shelley (1797-1851, nee Godwin) was born in Somers Town, near Euston, London. However, her mother died of puerperal poisoning only ten days after young Mary's birth, leaving the baby motherless for fours years until Godwin married again. Given her tragic start in life, it is no wonder death and birth are so interlinked in Frankenstein. Tragedy never seemed far away for Mary, as she was to later suffer the losses of three of her children and her husband, Percy, as well as of family friend, Lord Byron.

After Godwin's remarriage, Mary's misery continued, as her relationship with her father's new wife, Mrs Mary Jane Clairmont was strained. Mary's relationship with one of her step sisters was even worse.

Perhaps because of her problems with her new relations, Mary became exceptionally attached to her father, although she did not share his liberal, revolutionary political views. Until she met her future husband, the poet Percy Bysshe Shelley, she admitted her father was her 'God'. She was incredibly influenced by Godwin's Calvinist-influenced philosophy, believing that we learn from self-denial, disappointment and self-control.

Although Godwin's popularity declined as the nineteenth century progressed, Mary was still able to meet his eminent guests, such as the poet Samuel Taylor Coleridge, famous for the 'Rime of the Ancient Mariner', which is referred to in 'Frankenstein'.

Another influence on Mary was her future husband, Percy who, at the age of nineteen, began visiting Godwin with his young wife in May 1814. Percy was a political idealist, who hated tyranny and was drawn to Godwin's philosophy. Shelley donated a lot of money to Godwin, who was always ready to accept it, although he could never accept his daughter's elopement with a married man, which resulted in marriage by December 1816.

Before that, in July 1814, Percy took Mary and her allegedly poisonous step-sister Jane, who now called herself 'Claire' Clairmont on a trip to Europe. Upon their return at the end of that summer, Mary moved into Percy's rented lodgings, although he rarely was there as he was desperately trying to avoid his creditors.
By February 1815, Mary gave birth to her unnamed first child, who died a few days afterwards. Born the following year, her next child, William, whose name appears in 'Frankenstein' lasted only three and a half years.

Urged to go by her hated step-sister Claire (previously known as Jane), the still-unmarried Mary took William on her trip to Geneva, Switzerland with Percy. Originally, Percy's plan was to go to Italy, but Claire was having an affair with George Gordon, Lord Byron (1788-1824) and was desperate to continue it. The result was the writing of 'Frankenstein', as Mary attempted to take part in Byron's impromptu ghost-story writing competition during the wet weather.

Her initial attempts were doomed to failure, as she drew a blank. However, after overhearing Percy's conversation with John Polidori (Byron's personal doctor) on Dr Erasmus Darwin's view that creating life was not impossible, Mary found an idea which she could develop into the novel, which would become 'Frankenstein'. Darwin had published 'Zoonomia' in 1794, which discussed spontaneous generation.

Three years before that, Luigi Galvani published 'Commentary on the Effects of Electricity on Muscular Motion', which was about how an electric current can cause limbs of deceased animals to move, if applied to the body parts in question. These experiments also influenced Mary, as did Giovanni Adini's, as he took 'galvanism' a stage further, by electrifying the corpse of the hanged murderer George Forster, whose eye opened. Note that in Mary's novel, something similar happens to the monster after an electric current is administered.

Consequently, given the use of such content, it is not altogether surprising that 'Frankenstein' is often considered to be the very first science fiction novel. However, rather than expressing a positive view of science, Mary is critical of the typical Romantic hero's attempt to over-reach himself. In this case, that hero is Victor Frankenstein, who is obsessive in his desire to create life, which ironically only causes destruction. In this sense, she lacked her husband's idealism and belief in man's creative powers. In fact, some see the novel as a subtle criticism of her husband, especially as Percy often used the name Victor as a pseudonym. Additionally, Percy was known for his passion for reform and his almost obsessive enthusiasm for science and, in particular, chemistry, electricity and galvanism.

Most of all, Percy was a famous Romantic poet, so it is understandable that Mary was influenced. Although many critics now see 'Frankenstein' as a critique of Romanticism as opposed to a handbook for it, the protagonist is a Romantic hero who defies God by creating life. However, Victor's failure probably reflects Mary's view that domestic life is more important than an obsessive attempt by man to over-reach himself. Nevertheless, there are archetypal Romantic settings, like the Alps, which feature prominently in the novel.

Generically, although nearly all novels are regarded as hybrids, 'Frankenstein' is widely considered to be Gothic. Even this definition is problematic, as 'Frankenstein' differs from Gothic novels that preceded it, such as Horace Walpole's 'The Castle of Otranto' (1765). Walpole, in fact, maintained that Mary's father was 'one of the greatest monsters exhibited in history'. From this comment, we can see why Mary produced a monster who can elicit the reader's sympathy.

> Meanwhile, some critics believe that the character of Agatha may be based on her namesake who appears in Matthew Lewis's Gothic novel, 'The Monk' (1796). Nevertheless, the lack of ruined monasteries and castles as part of the setting makes the novel defy Gothic conventions. On the other hand, unspeakable horror does appear, which makes the novel appear Gothic, despite its reliance on science rather than the supernatural as a plot driver.

Gothic writers are also expected to include doppelgängers in their texts and, in this sense, Mary delivers. There are number of Gothic doubles in the text, none more so than Victor, who doubles up as his own monster. Of course, the monster represents the dark side of Victor's personality.

As well as that, the Gothic explores crossing forbidden boundaries and her husband, Percy, was guilty of that, just like Victor. To a lesser degree, perhaps, Walton has also over-reached himself by attempting to explore the North Pole. At the time when the novel was written, the British government were hoping to find a shorter passage to India and China via the Arctic, so a couple of dangerous expeditions had been prepared.

Meanwhile, some of Mary's other influences pre-date the Arctic expeditions. Philosophy was no stranger to the Godwin household, so it is unsurprising that Jean-Jacques Rousseau's ideas permeate the novel. The eighteenth-century Genevan maintained that man or woman would be happier if left in his or her natural state of freedom. He also believed that without companionship, a man or woman would be ostracised by society and become 'the most disfigured of all'. Clearly, Mary draws on this idea to create a monster, who starts off life with pure intentions (like Cervantes' 'Don Quixote') conforming to John Locke's tabula rasa (blank slate or erased tablet) theory, before turning malevolent in response to the prejudice and hatred he has to endure.

While Mary was influenced by Rousseau's philosophy, she was also under the spell of classic literature, such as John Milton's 'Paradise Lost'. There are a number of references to the epic poem about God's creation of Adam and Eve and how they were banished from the Garden of Eden because the ate the forbidden fruit from the Tree of Knowledge. In the novel, Victor is guilty of consuming too much knowledge and is similarly punished. Meanwhile, the monster reads the poem, while he is in hiding, comparing himself both to Satan and Adam.

As well as the Biblical story and Milton's take on it, Samuel Richardson's 'Clarissa' seems to have convinced Mary to use an epistolary form for her narrative.

Another book that Mary read was Charles Brockden Brown's 'Wieland' or 'The Transformation' (1798), which includes a reflective character called Carwin, who is almost a combination of Victor and the monster he creates.Other literary influences include Mary's own father William Godwin, who wrote 'Caleb Williams' (1794). The theme of pursuit could have been borrowed from the novel or possibly from Coleridge's 'Ancient Mariner', which includes the lines: 'a frightful fiend / Doth close behind him tread'. Meanwhile, the eponymous Caleb Williams claims his 'offense had merely been a mistaken thirst for knowledge', echoing Victor.

Arguably, the Greek mythological character of Prometheus is even more influential on 'Frankenstein'. The alternative title of the novel is 'The Modern Prometheus', who in the Greek original stole forbidden fire from the gods to give to mankind. The Romans changed Prometheus into a character who made man out of clay and water. Likewise, Victor defies the gods and creates a man.

Page-by-page analysis
Letter One
The epistolary novel quickly establishes its letter format through the use of Walton's framed narrative, through which all other narratives are embedded..

The reader experiences some realism in the place name St Petersburg, which is northern Russia, and the date: 'Dec. 11th,

17__'. The exact date is hidden, which implies that some aspects of the mystery about to unfold cannot be shared.

We soon realise that Walton has embarked on a madcap adventure, as he tells his sister that 'no disaster' has occurred yet, despite her 'evil forebodings' (15).

He is driven by the honourable desire to be beneficent, judging by the store he places on 'the inestimable benefit' which he 'shall confer on all mankind to the last generation, by discovering a passage near the [North] pole' (16). This highlights how unselfish Walton is, if we trust the reliability of this first-person narrator. Meanwhile, we can also tell that Walton is on a quest for personal 'glory', which he prefers to 'wealth' (17).

His letter ends melodramatically with rhetorical questions as he wonders how he can 'answer' the question regarding his 'return' date, while signing off rather formally as R.Walton (18). Clearly, their relationship is not only distant geographically.

Letter Two

Walton's continuing correspondence with his sister, Mrs Saville, reveals one of the novel's themes: loneliness. Walton admits that he 'bitterly' feels 'the want of a friend' (19). Although it has been suggested that Walton is a double for Frankenstein, in this way he differs from the protagonist, as Victor often prefers his own company, as we shall see later in the narrative.

However, both men are aloof from others, as Walton dismisses the 'rugged bosoms' of his shipmates and is sure he will 'find no friend on the wide ocean' (20). It is almost as if he thinks he is a cut above the common man.

Like Victor, Walton is determined to overcome the forces of nature. The captain is patiently waiting 'until the weather' will 'permit' his 'embarkation' (21). Both men share a resilience, which may make the capable of the impossible.

Once again, Walton closes the final paragraph of his letter with a rhetorical question: 'Shall I meet you again [...]?' (22). However, his growing intimacy with his sister is indicated by him signing off with his first name, 'Robert' (22).

Letter Three

By now, nearly eight months have passed since Walton's first letter to his sister and he claims that he is 'well advanced' on his 'voyage' (23). Unlike Shakespeare's Macbeth, Walton claims his men are 'firm of purpose' (23). It appear that he has every chance of success.

His increasing confidence is exemplified by the use of two rhetorical questions: 'Why not still proceed over the untamed yet obedient element? What can stop the determined heart and resolved will of man?' (24). This inner confidence may have been mirrored by the writer's partner, Percy Bysshe Shelley.

Walton signs off with initials this time, which may suggest that he is rushing towards his goal. He also uses an exclamation: 'Heaven bless my beloved sister!' which implies a depth of feeling not hitherto seen (24).

Letter Four

The 'thick fog' described in the opening of this letter to works as pathetic fallacy, as soon Walton will begin hearing the story of Frankenstein and his creation (25). At this stage, nothing is clear, but emerging out of the fog is 'a being' possessed 'of gigantic stature' (25). It later transpires that this giant is Victor Frankenstein's creation.

Walton's racist attitude which was prevalent at the time is apparent when he describes Victor Frankenstein, who is 'not as the other traveller seemed to be, a savage inhabitant of some undiscovered island, but an European' (26).This implies that Victor's creation could be a 'noble savage', which is a term that is credited to John Dryden, who wrote the play: 'The Conquest of Granada' (1672). In a sense, the monster could symbolise humanity's innate goodness. Regardless of that, it appears that Walton favours Victor, purely on racial appearances.

Walton appears to believe his gut instinct that Victor is on the side of moral correctness, as he relates how 'his whole countenance is lighter up [....] with a beam of benevolence and sweetness that I never saw equalled' (27). Through the use of hyperbole and an alliterative 'b', the writer emphasises how impressed Walton is with Victor.

The letter goes on to foreshadow the reanimation of dead parts by describing how 'a new spirit of life animated the decaying frame' of Victor (28). Walton appears preoccupied with this fascinating, new guest on board his ship and says he will continue his 'journal' when he has 'fresh incidents to record' (28). This makes Walton appear like a reliable narrator with journalistic intentions to document anything interesting concerning Victor.

Eight days later, Walton's next entry describes Victor as 'so noble a creature destroyed by misery', which makes Frankenstein appear as the perfect Gothic double of his creature (28).

The pursuit of knowledge is a theme explored in this letter, as Walton asserts that 'one man's life or death' is 'but a small price to pay for the acquirement of the knowledge' which he seeks (29). Victor's bitter experience forces him to condemn Walton as an 'unhappy man!' (29). Furthermore, Victor asks

Walton rhetorically: 'Do you share my madness? Have you drunk also of the intoxicating draught? (29). To further condemn the reckless pursuit of knowledge, Victor decides to 'reveal' his 'tale' (29). The writer cleverly uses Walton's ambition as a reason for Victor to relate his cautionary story to prevent another individual becoming embroiled in a catastrophic set of circumstances after trying to achieve an almost impossible individualistic ambition.

Six days after that journal entry, which appears in Walton's letter to his sister, Victor hopes 'that the gratification of' the Captain's 'wishes' will 'not be a serpent to sting' him (31). This is a clear reference to the biblical story of story of Adam and Eve, which saw God's children eating forbidden fruit from the Tree of Knowledge. This leads them to being expelled from the Garden of Eden. Similarly, Victor has been sentenced to eternal damnation on earth for his gall at trying to act creator, effectively defying God.

Meanwhile, Walton dutifully prepares 'to record, as nearly as possible in' Victor's 'own words', Frankenstein's story (31). This adds realism to the narative as Walton admits human unreliability.

Interestingly, the writer makes Walton seem so absorbed in Frankenstein's narrative that he forgets to sign off his letter. Using sound imagery, the writer tries to convey how rapt Walton is as he listens to Victor's 'full-toned voice', which 'swells in' his 'ears' (32).

Chapter One

The narrative voice switches to Victor, who starts his story at the beginning with a gradual exposition. He explains that he is 'Genevese', like Jean-Jacques Rousseau, whose philosophy lays the foundation for some of writer's core beliefs that are evident in the novel (33).

Victor reveals that his father's friend, Beaufort, has had to go to 'Lucerne' in order to live 'unknown and in wretchedness' after paying 'his debts' (33). The writer's husband, Percy, similarly had retreated from England to avoid paying his debts and was unable to settle in one place for a number of years due to financial problems.

Beaufort dies, leaving his daughter, Caroline behind. Victor's father comes to her aid 'like a protecting spirit' and 'two years after' the death Caroline becomes 'his wife' and Victor's mother (34). She is significantly younger and consequently Victor's father tries to 'shelter her, as a fair exotic is sheltered by the gardener' (35). This makes Caroline sound frail and fragile, foreshadowing her early death in the narrative.

Before her demise, Caroline chooses Elizabeth Lavenza as a foster child, due to her appearing to be 'heaven-sent' and 'of a different stock' to the 'vagrants' she lives with (36). This implies that the Frankensteins believe in elitism and blue blood, especially as the narrative mentions she is the 'daughter of a Milanese nobleman' (36).

Victor becomes possessive of Elizabeth, whom he regards as his to 'protect, love and cherish' (37). This triplet suggests a strength of feeling which is unmatched later by commitment, as Victor unwisely puts his scientific obsession before his family and friends and pays the ultimate price for doing so.

Chapter Two

The theme of seclusion is broached early on in the chapter, as Victor admits it is 'his temper to avoid a crowd, and to attach' himself 'fervently to a few' (38). The alliterative 'f' reminds the reader how close Victor must be to one of his only friends, Henry Clerval, who 'loved [...] danger for its own sake' (39). The pair seem to have recklessness in common.

Victor is also dependent on the companionship of Elizabeth, who is 'the living spirit of love', who prevents him becoming 'sullen in' his 'study' (40). The sibilance reminds the reader how

Victor might shun society and live in silence if Elizabeth is not there to keep him grounded.

Victor's passionate obsession with science is clearly expounded with the writer conveying it through figurative language describing the scientist Sir Isaac Newton as 'like a child picking up shells beside the great and unexplored ocean of truth' (41). The combination of a simile and metaphor conveys Victor's fascination for science and the glory of discovery.

Like Walton, Victor shuns 'wealth' as 'an inferior object', striving instead for 'glory', which 'would attend discovery' (42). Victor is, of necessity, self-taught as his father is 'not scientific' and he is 'left to struggle with a child's blindness' (42). The metaphoric use of 'blindness' makes the reader admire Victor's tenacity and determination to overcome all obstacles.

Despite his commitment to science, Victor appears to believe in 'Destiny', which is personified by the writer. Victor believes chance has 'decreed' his 'utter and terrible destruction' (43). This seems incredibly unscientific, but makes his reading of occult and alchemist writer's like 'Cornelius Agrippa, Albertus Magnus, and Paracelsus' seem more understandable (43).

Chapter Three

The writer appears to be heavily influenced by Romantic literature, judging by her choice of setting. After choosing Geneva, Rousseau's birthplace, Mary Shelley has her protagonist study at 'the university of Ingolstadt', the home of the eighteenth-century instigators of the 1789 French Revolution (44).

Victor then relates how his mother died, nursing Elizabeth. This narrative foreshadows the creation of his monster, as he describes how 'the brightness of a beloved eye can' be 'extinguished' (45). Death and life are inextricably linked, when

9-1 GCSE REVISION NOTES – FRANKENSTEIN

Victor creates his monster later in the narrative, with the description of an eye making the circle complete.

More foreshadowing is in evidence in the description of Clerval, who Victor reads in 'his kindling eye and in his animated glance a restrained but firm resolve, not to be chained to the miserable details of commerce' (46). Once again, the 'eye' is mentioned, which links Clerval to Frankenstein's creation.. Additionally, Clerval shares Walton and Victor's aversion to business and, presumably, money. Finally, like Victor and Walton, Clerval intends to defy his family in pursuit of what he wants.

As previously, when Victor attributes the future to 'Destiny', this time the narrative personifies 'Chance - or rather the evil influence, the Angel of Destruction' to the fact that he is led to M. Krempe (47). His belief in fate is far from scientific.

Unlike Krempe, another university lecturer, M. Waldman, is much more sympathetic to Victor. Waldman's voice is 'the sweetest' he 'had ever heard' (48). However, even he tells Victor that 'the elixir of life is a chimera' or something that is impossible to achieve (49). Waldman smiles 'at the names of Cornelius Agrippa and Paracelsus, but without the contempt that M. Krempe had exhibited' (50). This shows how out of touch with contemporary scientific thinking Frankenstein is, while highlighting how determined Victor is to achieve the what is considered unachievable.

Chapter Four

The narrative continues to explore the theme of seclusion and obsession, as Victor tells Walton how 'natural philosophy, and particularly chemistry, became nearly' his 'sole occupation' (51). By mentioning 'natural philosophy', Victor is referring to the science.

This lack of social interaction has led to Victor taking a strange interest in observing 'the natural decay and corruption of the human body' (52). The writer uses Manichaean imagery to further describe Victor's macabre fascination with 'how the worm inherited the wonders of the eye and brain [...] until from the midst of this darkness a sudden light broke in upon' him, as he discovers an 'astonishing [...] secret' (53). In effect, he sees the light, making him a God-like human being, who can bestow 'animation upon lifeless matter' (53).

The narrator echoes Mary Shelley's belief regarding 'how dangerous is the acquirement of knowledge and how much happier that man is who believes his native town to be the world, than he who aspires to be greater than his nature will allow' (54). The writer is clearly trying to warn of the dangers of being overly ambitious.

Nevertheless, Victor relates how the pursuit of his breathtaking discovery led him to a 'variety of feelings which bore' him 'onwards, like a hurricane' (55). The natural simile suggests someone out of control, dangerous and potentially destructive.

This single obsession possesses Victor so much that his 'eyes' become 'insensible to the charms of nature' (56). In effect, he becomes isolated and unfeeling as a result of his passionate pursuit of his discovery.

The chapter ends with foreboding, as Victor relates that 'the leaves of that year had withered before' his 'work drew to a close' (57). The autumn leaves signify death, which is ironic as Victor is attempting to create life.

Chapter Five

The next chapter resumes Victor's narrative, as he informs Walton of how, 'on a dreary night of November', he sees 'the dull yellow eye of the creature open' (58). Initially, Victor seems in a proud, self-congratulatory mood, as he repeats the word 'beautiful' when initially describing his creature, whose 'hair was of a lustrous black, and flowing; his teeth of pearly whiteness' (58). However, it quickly dawns on Victor that 'these luxuriances only formed a horrid contrast with his watery eyes', 'his shrivelled complexion and straight black lips' (58). Before that, Victor mentions how the creature's 'yellow skin scarcely covered the work of muscles and arteries beneath', which suggests that he is quick to note the shortcomings of his creation (58).

Victor tells Walton his 'heart was 'filled' with 'breathless horror and disgust', as he was 'unable to endure the aspect of the being' he 'had created' (58). He retires to bed, where he dreams of Elizabeth, whose lips become 'livid with the hue of death' after he imprints 'the first kiss on her lips' (59). Clearly, Victor associates love and procreation with death and this is further emphasised by him dreaming that he 'held the corpse of' his 'dead mother' in his 'arms', while noting 'the grave-worms crawling in the folds' of the shroud (59). The explicitness of the account of the vivid nightmare makes it clear how revolted Victor feels regarding what he has created.

When he awakes, Victor discovers that the 'eyes, if eyes they may be called' of 'the miserable monster' are 'fixed' on him (59). The creature's 'grin' that 'wrinkled his cheeks' and 'hand', which is 'stretched out' indicate that 'the demoniacal corpse' does not intend to cause Victor harm (59). Nevertheless, Victor escapes, rushing 'downstairs', which might symbolise that he is morally travelling ever nearer to hell (59) Mirroring the writer's reading, Victor describes the creature as 'a thing such as even Dante could not have conceived' (59).

The writer uses pathetic fallacy to show the protagonist's emotions, as 'morning, dismal and wet, at length' dawns (60). Victor's fear is emphasised by the intertextual link to Coleridge's 'Ancient Mariner' poem that scared her partner, Percy, so much. Victor knows that 'a frightful fiend / Doth close behind him tread' (60).

Clerval's arrival gives Victor so respite and 'delight', with his friend implying ignorance is bliss by quoting from Oliver Goldsmith's 'The Vicar of Wakefield', whose 'Dutch schoolmaster' claims: 'I have ten thousand florins a year without Greek' (60, 61). In other words, it is possible to thrive without knowledge.

Victor appears to be nearly insane as he relates that Clerval sees 'a wildness' in his 'eyes for which he' cannot 'account' and notes his 'loud, unrestrained, heartless laughter' (62). The triplet emphasises how Victor has almost completely lost his self-control.

The narrator admits he is 'very ill', but he is on the way to recovery when he perceives 'that the fallen leaves had disappeared and that the young buds were shooting forth from the trees' in a 'divine spring' (63). It reminds the reader that there may be an almighty creator with greater powers than Victor.

Now that Clerval can converse with Victor again, he mentions 'a letter that had been lying' there for 'some days' from his 'cousin', Elizabeth (64). In this 1831 revision of the original text written eighteen years previously, Elizabeth is not a blood relation of Victor. This revision leaves the text less open to criticism on the subject of incest.

Chapter Six

In Elizabeth's embedded narrative, she almost immediately establishes that she is the ideal nineteenth-century woman, wishing to nurse Victor back to health with extra 'care and attention' (65).

She then relates the tale of Justine, who is compared to the beautiful 'Angelica' character, who appears in Ariosto's 'Orlando Furioso' (1516) (66). Diminutive language like 'little' increases the reader's sympathy for Justine, who ironically will not receive justice later in the narrative, despite her name sharing the same root prefix.

Elizabeth also discusses the ill-fated younger brother of Victor, William, who is described as possessing 'sweet laughing blue eyes, dark eyelashes, and curling hair' (68). The writer is creating sympathy in the readers for both characters, so that when they meet their demise, more of the horror of the crimes against them sink in.

Once Victor has finished reading the letter, he relates how traumatised he is at 'the sight of a chemical instrument' (69). He appears to be mentally disturbed by what he has done.

Meanwhile, we discover how Clerval is completely different to Victor in some ways, in that he wants to make himself 'complete master of the Oriental languages' (70). For the sake of 'temporary amusement', Victor takes an interest too (70). In time, Victor becomes 'the same happy creature who, a few years ago, loved and beloved by all, had no sorrow or case' (71). The use of hyperbole implies that Victor is deceiving himself to some extent. Interestingly, he describes himself as a 'creature', which links him with the monster. However, it appears that he has made a full recovery, as he bounds 'along with feelings of unbridled joy and hilarity' upon returning to 'college on a Sunday afternoon' (72). The fact that the time setting is on a Sunday may imply that he has returned to conventionality and is grounded once more.

Chapter Seven

The next embedded narrative is Alfonse Frankenstein's, as Victor's father's letter is read by the son upon his return to university.

The first thing to note is the use of the oxymoron 'cruel kindness' to not inform Victor of the family's misfortune' (73). Two exclamations reveal all: 'William is dead!' and 'he is murdered!' (73).

The word 'livid' is used once more to describe death, as William is 'stretched on the grass livid and motionless' (74). Livid connotes anger as well as bruising, which is apt given he bears 'the print of the murderer's finger was on his neck' (74).

Clerval sees how Victor is emotionally devastated by the news and the writer has him asking the following rhetorical question: 'are we always to be unhappy?' (75). This could convince the reader that Victor is so unfortunate in normal circumstances, but it is dramatic irony as Clerval is unaware that his friend is the architect of his doom.

In his 'melancholy', Victor finds himself unable to get past 'Lausanne, in this painful state of mind' (76). Referring to Lord Byron's 'Childe Harold's Pilgrimage', the writer has Victor noting that 'the snowy mountains, "the palaces of nature", were not changed' (76). It reminds the reader that Victor is a Byronic hero, with little regard for scientific authority, while nature's power continues, despite the frightful personal circumstances that Victor must endure.

Victor continues his journey to 'the environs of Geneva', he watches a 'tempest, so beautiful yet terrific' (77). Like a Romantic writer, Mary Shelley seems in awe of the elements. Meanwhile, Victor sees 'a figure which stole from behind a clump of trees' (77). Of course, like Victor, we can guess that it is the monster who is responsible for William's death and the unspeakable description of his pain is melodramatically Gothic, as he is 'forced to lean against a tree for support' (78).

Once he gets back his 'father's house' at 'about five in the morning', he gazes at 'the picture of' his 'mother' (79). She is portrayed 'kneeling by the coffin of her dead father' (79). It is almost as if the Frankensteins are preoccupied with tragedy, as it brings out 'an air of dignity and beauty' (79). Similarly, Mary Shelley had to deal with the death of her mother, who died shortly after giving birth to her.

The tragedy increases once Victor discovers through Ernest's rhetorical question that Justine has been accused of 'so appalling a crime' (80). Ernest's persuasive device expresses the incredulity felt that Justine could have killed William. Meanwhile, also using a rhetorical question, Victor persuades himself that he is to blame for unleashing 'rash ignorance [...] upon the world' (81).

However, Victor rashly believes he can ensure Justine's 'acquittal', which calms the distraught Elizabeth, while Alfonse tells her to 'rely on the justice of our laws' (82). Mary Shelley seems to be of the view that there is little to no justice in the world, judging by the tragic verdict later in the narrative.

Chapter Eight

Victor's self-pity continues as he says he is 'the cause' for Justine's bleak future, which is to be 'an ignominious grave' (83). He is so self-absorbed that he cannot see past himself. He is also filled with pessimism.

However, Justine takes centre stage as it is her trial in court that we witness, albeit through Victor's perspective. The use of the tricolon: 'surprise, horror, and misery' reminds the reader how affected Justine is by the false accusation.

We now hear how she looked for William at night but as 'the gates of Geneva were shut [...] she was forced to remain several hours of the night in a barn belonging to a cottage' (85). Like the monster, when he finds himself in a hovel next to the DeLacy's home, Justine is sleeping rough. Like him, she is about to be unjustly treated.

Although Elizabeth's testimony is designed to save her, it backfires. This is because the guilt seems to reside in 'the bauble' taken from William which is found on Justine (86). Therefore, the Elizabeth's assertion that she would 'have willingly give it to her' makes Justine appear guilty of 'the blackest ingratitude' (86).

Once again, Victor is completely self-absorbed. He states that 'the tortures of the accused did not equal' his, as 'the fangs of remorse tore' his 'bosom' (86). The figurative language shows how sorry Victor feels for himself, although it is Justine is 'condemned' to death (87). She later 'confessed' to the crime, as she was 'threatened' with 'excommunication' from the church (87, 88). This reminds us that in the nineteenth century, many people feared eternal damnation more than anything.

Victor's reaction to the news is animal-like and somewhat reminiscent of his creation, as he admits he 'gnashed' his 'teeth' (89). The following day, we are spared the details as she 'perished on the scaffold as a murderess!' The exclamation shows how guilty Victor feels about what has happened.

Chapter Nine

Volume Two begins with Victor's self-absorption, as he relates how his 'blood flowed freely in' his 'veins', although 'a weight of despair and remorse pressed on' his 'heart' (93). The writer's use of figurative language reminds us that Victor is focused on his own reaction to events rather than on the other people involved and damaged by what he has created.

He retires to the family house 'at Belrive', which means beautiful shore, when translated into English (94). It could make the reader feel less sympathy for Victor, as he has somewhere 'agreeable' to go to, although he contemplates suicide (94). When he thinks of 'the heroic and suffering Elizabeth' and his 'father and surviving brother', he thinks again (94).

Victor's anger is evident, as his eyes become 'inflamed' and he gnashes his teeth, stating that he 'would have made a pilgrimage to the highest peak of the Andes' if he felt he could 'extinguish' the life of his creation (95). Interestingly, the writer uses the word 'pilgrimage', which has religious connotations. As a mad scientist who has created life, Victor has completely gone against religious belief in an almighty creator.

Elizabeth's speech to Victor is just as 'Romantic' with a capital 'R', as she feels 'as if' she 'were walking on the edge of a precipice' (96). It brings to mind the famous Romantic painting by Caspar David Friedrich entitled: 'Wanderer above the Sea of Fog' (1818). Similarly, Victor's summer 'wanderings' are soon directed towards the valley of Chamounix', where he hears 'the sound of the river raging among the rocks' (97). The alliterative sound of the river reminds us of how furious Victor is at his creation and how his blood is pumping through his veins in his efforts to find his creature. The personification of 'Sleep', which 'crept over' him, shows how feeble his exertions are compared to the forces of nature, which always overwhelm human beings (98).

Chapter Ten

The writer's Romantic influences are revealed as Victor's narrative describes how the 'glorious presence-chamber of imperial Nature' is 'broken only by the brawling waves or the fall of some vast fragment' (99). Nature, personified, is portrayed as powerful and awe-inspiring.

In a reference to her father, William Godwin, and his 'doctrine of necessity', the writer has Victor asking rhetorically: 'why does man boast of sensibilities superior to those apparent in the brute; it only renders them more necessary beings' (100). More intertextuality is evident as Mary Shelley includes an extract from her husband's poem entitled: 'Mutability'. Both references indicate Romantic influences on the protagonist, who is doomed to 'wand'ring' like Percy Bysshe Shelley's speaker (101).

After arriving 'at the top' of the summit of Montanvert, Victor beholds 'the figure of a man [...] advancing towards' him 'with superhuman speed' (101). Victor threatens the creature, once he arrives, saying he will 'trample' him 'to dust' (102).

The creature is undaunted, saying he 'ought to be' Victor's 'Adam', but instead he is treated like 'the fallen angel' (103). He is determined to tell his 'tale' and, although Victor repeats the word 'cursed', he allows his 'odious companion' to begin (103).

Chapter Eleven

The creature begins his tale and we immediately feel some sympathy, given it is a first-person perspective and that he is inundated with sensations as he 'saw, felt, heard and smelt at the same time' (105). We can imagine his confusion at feeling so much all at once.

He adds that he was 'a poor, helpless, miserable wretch', who has enough sensibility to appreciate the beauty of the moon, which his narrative describes poetically as 'a radiant form' (105-6, 106). His association with the moon makes him appear to be a creature of the night.

However, his mind is not evil. Instead, it is more like a tabula rasa or blank slate upon which experiences will be written and learnt from. The idea is taken from the philosophy of John Locke (1632-1704). The proof of that is the creature thrusting his 'hand into the live embers' of a fire (107). He pays the price for his ignorance, but we sense he will learn from it.

The creature continues his poetic narrative, relating how entering a shepherd's hut felt as 'divine a retreat as Pandaemonium appeared to the daemons of hell after their sufferings in the lake of fire' in John Milton's 'Paradise Lost' (108).

Our sympathy for the outcast increases as he 'fearfully' takes 'refuge in a low hovel' (109). He describes it as his 'kennel', which further emphasises how he has been treated like a dog or worse by Victor (109).

From his hovel, the creature can spy on the family next door through 'a small and almost imperceptible chink' (110). He particularly admires the 'old man', who can 'produce sounds sweeter than the voice of the thrush or nightingale' on his instrument (110). The juxtaposition of the family life, which the writer clearly approves of, against the enforced solitude which the creature endures, makes his loneliness seem all the more abhorrent. He appreciates the old man's 'benevolence and love', qualities that are missing from his life (111).

The younger man begins 'to utter sounds that' are 'monotonous', which he later realises is reading aloud (112). The creature clearly is impressionable and eager to learn as much as he can from his neighbours.

Chapter Twelve

Like Justine, the creature lays on 'straw' and, also like her, he only receives injustice (113). Additionally, the straw bed is reminiscent of the biblical story of Jesus Christ, who is laid in a manger at birth as there is no room at the inns in Bethlehem. Similarly, the creature has had a tough start to life and, understandably, feels 'wretched' (113).

The creature is presented in a similar way to Shakespeare's outsider, Caliban, in 'The Tempest', as the two share as similar diet of 'berries, nuts, and roots' as well as poetic expressiveness (114).

The creature is still learning from his neighbours, as he analyses how 'the words they spoke sometimes produced pleasure or pain, smiles or sadness' (115). This gives him the motivation 'to become acquainted' with this 'godlike science' (115).

The family's innocence is exemplified by Felix carrying 'with pleasure to his sister the first little white flower that peeped out from beneath the snowy ground' (116). White symbolises purity, amongst other things.

Meanwhile, the creature forms in his 'imagination a thousand pictures of presenting' himself to his neighbours (117). The imagination is much revered by Romantic writers, although the creature turns out to be falsely optimistic.

He is more accurate when he compares his situation to that of Jean de La Fontaine's (1621-1695) re-telling of Aesop's fable of the 'ass and the lap-dog' (118). In the fable, the ass attempts to be as affectionate as the lap-dog, but is beaten with a stick for his troubles.

Chapter Thirteen

Mirroring the creature's hopes for the future, the season begins to change as 'spring advanced rapidly' (119).

He continues to watch the family, noting the arrival of Safie 'on horseback' with her 'hair of a shining raven black' (119). The raven usually symbolises death. Felix's possessiveness of her is reminiscent of Victor's feelings towards Elizabeth, as he calls her 'his sweet Arabian' (120). When she sings she is 'like a nightingale of the woods' (121). Through the use of a simile, the writer conveys the creature's admiration for Safie.

The creature continues to learn as he listens to Felix teaching Safie from 'Volney's "Ruins of Empires"' (122). From that, he picks up racial prejudice, as Asiatics are described as 'slothful', especially in comparison to the 'stupendous genius and mental activity of the Grecians' (122). At the time, grouping people according to racial stereotypes was not uncommon and the monster, for all his intelligence, does not question it.

However, he does realise that knowledge is a curse as well as a blessing, as the writer has him describe it as 'like a lichen on the rock' (123). He sometimes wishes to 'shake off all feeling and thought' as he realises that 'sorrow only increased with knowledge' (123). It only makes him question his lack of 'friends and relations, with the writer increasing the reader's sympathy for him through the use of rhetorical questions like: 'What was I?' (124).

Chapter Fourteen

The creature goes on to relate the tale of Safie's father, who is the victim of injustice like Justine and the monster. Safie's father was 'tried and condemned to death' for a reason that the creature 'could not learn' (125). The creature assumes the reason concerns 'his religion and wealth rather than the crime alleged against him' (125).

Safie's mother 'was a Christian Arab, seized and made a slave by the Turks' (126). However, she teaches Safie 'to aspire to higher powers of intellect and an independence of spirit forbidden to the female followers of Mahomet (127). This is reminiscent of the views of the writer's mother, Mary Wollstonecraft, who wrote 'A Vindication of the Rights of Woman'.

Felix, meanwhile, helps Safie's father to escape and is only rewarded with the 'deceit' of the 'treacherous Turk' (128). The alliteration emphasises how awfully behaved Safie's father is, particularly as he plans 'a residence in Turkey' for his daughter, which is 'abhorrent to her' (128, 129).

Chapter Fifteen

The creature puts the family on a pedestal, admiring 'their virtues' while remaining critical of 'the vices of mankind' (130).

He continues his education, reading 'Paradise Lost', 'Plutarch's Lives' and the 'Sorrows of Werter' (130). However, it only serves to make him apply his newly acquired knowledge to his 'own feelings and condition' (131). He believes that he is 'wretched, helpless, and alone' and more like Satan than Adam (132). We can see his destiny appears to be to follow a path of evil rather than the one of righteousness.

Although Felix and Agatha are 'not rich', they are 'assisted in their labours by servants' (133). He continues to compare their condition to his and concludes that he is 'a wretched outcast' with 'no Eve' to sooth his 'sorrows' and share his 'thoughts' (133, 134).

By now 'winter' has 'advanced', so it appears that the creature is unlikely to be able to find warmth from human company at such a bleak time in the calendar (134). Nevertheless, as soon as Safie, Agatha, and Felix depart 'on a long country walk', and the servants go 'to a neighbouring fair', the creature seizes the opportunity to talk to the blind old man (135).

He explains that he is 'a detestable monster' and sobs aloud (136). However, Felix returns to strike him 'violently with a stick' (137). Rather than retaliate and tear him 'limb from limb, as the lion tends the antelope', the creature's self-control is admirable as he returns to his 'hovel' (137).

Chapter Sixteen

The creature begins the chapter with the alliterative exclamation: 'Cursed, cursed creator!' (138). He follows it up with the rhetorical question: 'Why did I live?' (138). These opening sentences highlight how desperate the creature has become and how angry he is at his creator, especially after Felix's attack on him.

Like his creator, Victor, the creature defines emotion by his bodily reaction when he states that 'the fever of my blood did not allow me to be visited by peaceful dreams' (139). Again, his comments bear a marked similarity to those of his creator, when he admits 'feelings of revenge and hatred filled my bosom' (140).

He resolves to Victor's 'native town', Geneva, 'late in autumn' (141). The time setting indicates that death is not far away.

However, we feel some sympathy for the homeless creature who, without 'shelter', feels the 'hard and chill, and bare' 'surface of the earth' (142). This sympathy is increased as he saves a young girl from a 'rapid stream' and is shot (143). The 'hellish rage and gnashing of teeth' makes him appear like his creator, who is described similarly by the writer (143).

The creature next encounter with mankind is with 'a beautiful child', who turns out to be William (144). He suffers insults such as 'ugly wretch' and 'ogre' before he grasps the boy's 'throat to silence him' (144). Judging by his account, the death has occurred almost accidentally.

He then takes a 'glittering' 'portrait of a most lovely woman' from William's 'breast' (144). Next, the devious creature cleverly places 'the portrait securely in one of the folds' of

Justine's 'dress', who he finds sleeping in a barn (145). He guesses correctly that the 'punishment' will 'be hers' (145).

After this admission of guilt, it is unlikely that Victor will feel sympathy for the creature. Nevertheless, the monster requests 'a companion', who 'must be of the same species, and have the same defects' (146).

Chapter Seventeen

We return to Victor's narrative as, using a rhetorical question, he asks: 'Shall I create another like yourself, whose joint wickedness might desolate the world?' (147).

Nevertheless, the creature remains adamant that he needs a companion and rationally states that he is 'malicious because' he is 'miserable' (147). He is arguably more persuasive than his creator, as he asks rhetorically: 'Am I not shunned and hated by all mankind?'

Victor admits he 'was moved' by the monster's entreaties (148). He even calls his creation 'a creature of fine sensation' (148). However, as the conversation continues, Victor's 'feelings were altered to those of horror and hatred' (149). Nevertheless, Victor agrees to meet the creature's 'demand', as long as he carries out his 'solemn oath to quit Europe forever' (150).

The volume and the chapter end on a Gothic note, as we hear how Victor's feelings are indescribable: 'I cannot describe to you how the eternal twinkling of the stars weighed upon me' (151). He is silently committed to creating another monster and is unable to speak of it.

Chapter Eighteen

Like William Wordsworth's speaker in 'The Prelude', Victor takes 'a little boat' out on a 'lake alone' (155). He is at one with nature and in 'perfect solitude', clinging to 'every pretence of delay' rather than commencing work on a companion for his creature (155).

The dangers of solitude are noted by Alfonse Frankenstein, who admonishes his 'unhappy' son, who 'still' avoids his family's 'society' (156). The writer would not approve of such behaviour.

Even 'immediate' marriage with Elizabeth fills Victor with 'horror and dismay', so preoccupied is he with what he has to do (157). Metaphorically, he feels a 'deadly weight yet hanging round' his 'neck', which links him to Coleridge's albatross from 'Ancient Mariner' (157). Until he has completed this work, and 'enfranchised' himself from his 'miserable slavery', he feels he cannot 'claim Elizabeth' (158). Much of the language smacks of self-absorption, which the writer may want us to think is the result of seclusion.

Nevertheless, Victor's obsessive nature is unchanged, with his 'fixed and unobserving' eyes. (159). Like his creation, he cannot enjoy his life, and he similarly describes himself as 'a miserable wretch, haunted by a curse that shut up every avenue to enjoyment' (160).

As Victor travels to England, he appreciates the positive outlook of his friend, Clerval, whom is described using a line from Leigh Hunt's 'The Story of Rimini' (1816) as 'a being formed in the "very poetry of nature"' (161). Victor describes this 'tribute to the unexampled worth of Henry' as a 'gush of sorrow', which foreshadows the latter's death.

Chapter Nineteen

The travelogue continues, as Victor and Clerval disembark in London. As much as Victor tries to find 'a transitory peace', metaphorically he feels 'an insurmountable barrier placed between' him and 'his fellow-men' (163). The 'barrier' has been 'sealed with the blood of William and Justine' (163). Once again, Victor is presented as self-absorbed.

We quickly get a sense that for all his guilt, Victor is likely to make a similar mistake in the future. Even in the company of his best friend, Clerval, Victor appears to be mentally distant. Once again, Victor chooses solitude, alleging another engagement, that' he 'might remain alone' (164).

The pair continue to travel, proceeding 'to Oxford' (165). Victor remarks that the city remained loyal to Charles I during the English Civil War, although ultimately the loyalty did not alter the bloody outcome. Similarly, the reader gets a sense that Clerval's loyalty will be in vain.

As the two travel north, they stop at Matlock, in Derbyshire. Even the scenery has a doppelgänger, as Victor is reminded of Servox and Chamounix in Switzerland, by the 'wondrous cave' and its 'curiosities' (166). He cannot escape the fact that he is defying nature and its wonders by creating an abomination.

Victor's fears increase as the pair continue to journey north. He fears 'the daemon's disappointment', thinking he might 'wreak his vengeance on' his 'relatives' (167). Like the creature, 'this idea pursued' him (167). The personification makes it seem as if Victor is capable of tormenting himself, even in the creature's absence.

Eventually, Victor decides to 'finish' his 'work in solitude' in 'some remote part of Scotland' (168). Similar to the monster's skin, the 'remotest of the Orkneys' have 'hills' that 'are covered with veins' (168, 169). 'Immersed in solitude', Victor's work is described as 'considerably advanced' and therefore near completion (169). However, the protagonist dreads the consequences and the thought of them make his 'heart sicken in' his 'bosom' (169).

Chapter Twenty

The setting sun is appropriate as Victor does not 'have sufficient light' to continue his work (170). It appears that he is about to unleash the forces of darkness with his latest creation, who 'might become ten times more malignant than her mate'

(170). The alliteration combined with the hyperbole give us a sense of the horror in Victor's heart.

Victor reflects on how he has 'been moved by the sophisms of the being' into creating a mate (171). A sophism refers to an argument designed to deceive and the creature seems adept at using his eloquence to manipulate Victor. However, Victor realises his mistake and tears his latest creation 'to pieces' (171).

The protagonist's fears of reprisals are heightened by the sound imagery of the approaching creature, as Victor's 'ear' is 'suddenly arrested by the paddling of oars' (171).

The role reversal is complete as the creature asks Victor rhetorically: 'Do you dare break your promise?' (172). Additionally, the monster's commanding imperative: 'I am your master - obey!' makes it appear as if power has shifted, making Victor powerless by comparison (172). Before leaving, the creature makes the threat: 'I shall be with you on your wedding-night' (173).

There is something monstrous about Victor's reaction, as he admits he 'walked about the isle like a restless spectre' (174). Nevertheless, although he is worried, he feels that 'for the first time', he can see 'clearly' (175). The weather soon mirrors his increasing pessimism, as he chooses solitude in a small boat, as 'clouds hid the moon' and 'everywhere was obscure' (176). The conditions indicate that he cannot divine the future.

He lands in an inhospitable place, receiving a 'rude' 'answer from a stranger' (177). He is experiencing a similar reaction to his creature, who has been unwelcome wherever he has gone. Like Justine, Victor finds himself accused a crime: 'the death of a gentleman who was found murdered' (178).

Chapter Twenty-One

Victor is introduced to Mr Kirwin, who was mentioned in the
last chapter. He is described as 'an old benevolent man, with
calm and mild manners' (179). Judging by appearances, Victor
may have a chance of receiving justice from this magistrate.
Nevertheless, Victor's reaction, needing 'to lean on a chair for

support' when 'the mark of the fingers' of the creature are mentioned, make him seem culpable (180).

Victor's shock is intensified when he realises the murdered man is none other than 'Henry Clerval' (181). The protagonist succumbs to 'a fever' and questions rhetorically: 'Why did I not die?' (181).

When he regains consciousness, he feels rejected and accused like his creature, as he turns 'with loathing from' the hired nurse, who believes that he is guilty (182). Although Mr Kirwin shows Victor 'extreme kindness', Victor wonders whether or not he should 'declare' himself 'guilty' (183). The writer's use of hyperbolic alliteration makes Victor appear incredibly self-pitying, when he says he has 'become the most miserable of mortals' (183).

Victor continues to act melodramatically, as puts 'a hand before' his 'eyes', and cries 'out in agony' about the thought of a visitor (184). He mistakenly believes it is the creature, when it is, in fact, his father.

He tells his father that 'some destiny of the most horrible kind hangs over' him (185). This sounds irrational and completely unscientific. However, Victor is overcome with negative emotions, as he metaphorically states that: 'the cup of life was poisoned forever' (186). His belief in fate seems to have paralysed him and made him ill, as he reveals he is 'a mere skeleton', who is 'possessed by a kind of nightmare' (187).

Chapter Twenty-Two

Victor continues his self-indulgent narrative, as he tells the listening Walton: 'William, Justine, and Henry - they all died by my hands' (189). However, he cannot tell his father about the creature, so he admits he metaphorically 'chained' his 'tongue' (190).

Another embedded narrative moves the plot forwards, as Victor tells Walton about the contents of Elizabeth's letter. Her opening salutation is incredibly formal: 'My Dear Friend' (191). It makes the reader question whether her love for Victor is a passionate, romantic love or not. She continues to refer to Victor as her 'friend' throughout and asks him if he loves 'another' (192).

Nevertheless, Victor's possessiveness makes him consider Elizabeth to be 'a treasure', which he owns (193). The writer uses sibilance to show how she influences Victor, who admits 'some softened feelings stole into' his 'heart' (193). He writes back to her in an authoritative way, with imperatives such as: 'Chase away your idle fears' (193). His last line to her sounds incredibly domineering: 'I know you will comply' (194).

Fearing the creature's vengeance, Victor metaphorically feels his 'heart sink' as his 'marriage' draws 'nearer' (195). His masculine paranoia gets the better of him, as keeps 'pistols and a dagger constantly about' him (196). However, as 'the sun sank lower in the heavens' on his wedding day, we expect the creature to appear (197).

Chapter Twenty-Three

Pathetic fallacy makes it clear that Victor is expecting the worst as 'suddenly a heavy storm of rain descended' (198). While he paces up and down 'the passages of the house' looking for his adversary, the creature makes short work of Elizabeth, leaving 'her head hanging down, and her pale and distorted features half covered by her hair' (199). Like all the previous murders, 'the murderous mark of the fiend's grasp was on her neck' (199).

Victor sees the creature, who seems 'to jeer, as with a fiendish finger he' points 'towards the corpse of' his 'wife' (200). The creature leaps into the lake to elude a bullet from Victor's pistol. Victor hires a boat to pursue the creature, but he realises that the 'fiend had snatched [...] every hope of future happiness' from him (201).

The shocking murder of Elizabeth causes Victor's father to become 'unable to rise from his bed' and he follows her to the grave (202).

Victor tries to enlist the help of a local magistrate, telling him the creature 'may be hunted like the chamois, and destroyed as a beast of prey' (203). The narrator describes his 'rage' as 'unspeakable', which links the horrific murder directly with the Gothic genre (204).

Chapter Twenty-Four

The writer continues to portray Victor as a hot-blooded individual, who cannot keep his rage in check. Victor's rage is personified as he tells Walton: 'I was hurried away by fury' (205). This motivates him to pursue the creature, although he appears to be an unreliable narrator when he claims that 'fury' endowed him with 'composure' and 'allowed' him 'to be calculating and calm' (205).

Victor sounds like Lady Macbeth, who asks 'murdering ministers' to make her merciless, when he calls upon the 'wandering ministers of vengeance, to aid and conduct' him in his 'work' (206). His determination is not in doubt, as 'cold, want, and fatigue' are 'the least pains which' he is 'destined to endure' (207). The tricolon indicates that these basic obstacles are stacked up against him and his pursuit of the creature. The 'scoffing' of the 'devil' only heightens Victor's determination to catch the creature (208). He claims his 'courage and perseverance' are 'invigorated by' the 'scoffing words' of the creature (209).

Despite his desperation, Victor continues to hope for success. The writer personifies hope to show how much the protagonist believes in it: 'the continual protraction of hope, returning back upon the heart, often wrung bitter drops of despondency and grief from my eyes' (210). It appears that Victor is struggling internally to keep going.

He is also up against the elements, as 'the wind arose; the sea roared; and, as with the mighty shock of an earthquake, it split, and cracked' (211). Victor is 'left drifting on a scattered piece of ice' (211). It appears as if he has no chance of catching the creature. The writer's use of awe-inspiring natural imagery makes the novel appear to be paying homage to the Romantic movement.

Before Victor finishes his account, he warns Walton of the creature's 'eloquent and persuasive' words (212).

Walton continues the account on 'August 26th, 17__', asking his sister rhetorically whether or not her blood 'curdles' like his (212).

Not heeding Victor's warning, Walton 'sometimes' endeavours 'to gain from Frankenstein the particulars of his creature's formation' (213). Victor replies with a rhetorical question: 'Are you mad, my friend?' (213). The persuasive language prevents Walton from continuing this pursuit of forbidden knowledge. Victor compares himself to 'the archangel who aspired to omnipotence' and ended up 'chained in an eternal hell' (214). Now Victor has lost all hope of happiness, and that is conveyed in the following rhetorical question: 'Can any man be to me as Clerval was; or any woman another Elizabeth?' (215).

Walton breaks Victor's speech up by adding another date to his journal: 'September 2nd' (215). Like Victor, he blames other people's misfortunes on himself: 'If we are lost, my mad schemes are the cause' (215).

Victor's eloquence, which is reminiscent of the creature, serves to motivate the crew, who 'believe these vast mountains of ice are molehills' (216). The writer appears to recognise the power of words, while warning the reader to beware self-delusion.

When 'mutiny' threatens the expedition, Victor turns on the crew with a series of rhetorical questions, before using the following imperative: 'Do not return to your families with the stigma of disgrace marked on your brows' (216, 217). The writer shows how persuasive Victor is by allowing him to use direct address and figurative language to get the crew to continue the journey.

The dates begin to appear more frequently in the journal, as Walton tells his sister: 'The die is cast'. This implies that fate is against his expedition, which may be partly why he has 'consented to return' (218). Unlike Walton and his crew, Victor is not prepared to 'give up' as he claims that his 'purpose' is 'assigned' to him 'by Heaven' (219). However, he cannot complete his mission as 'his eyes closed forever' (220).

Over the dead Victor's body hangs 'a form', which Walton 'cannot find words to describe' (221). Defying description is one of the hallmarks of the Gothic genre.

The creature uses rhetorical questions to persuade Walton that he is not as evil as Victor claimed, saying: 'Think you that the groans of Clerval were music to my ears?' (222). However, the creature also admits that 'Evil [...] became my good', echoing Milton's 'Paradise Lost' (222).

Through the use of an analogy, the writer portrays Walton using persuasive language of his own to show that the creature is morally wrong: 'You throw a torch into a pile of buildings; and when they are consumed, you sit along the ruins, and lament the fall' (223).

The creature matches Victor's self-pity after he admits his crimes: 'your abhorrence cannot equal that with which I regard myself' (224). He looks forward to death stating: 'I shall ascend my funeral pile triumphantly, and exult in the agony of the torturing flames' (225). Although we do not see him die, we are told the creature is 'lost in darkness and distance' in Walton's narrative. The alliterative ending adds emphasis, making it sound as if the creature will carry out his suicidal wish.

Useful information/Glossary

Allegory: extended metaphor, like the grim reaper representing death, e.g. Scrooge symbolizing capitalism.

Alliteration: same consonant sound repeating, e.g. 'She sells sea shells'.

Allusion: reference to another text/person/place/event.

Ascending tricolon: sentence with three parts, each increasing in power, e.g. 'ringing, drumming, shouting'.

Aside: character speaking so some characters cannot hear what is being said. Sometimes, an aside is directly to the audience. It's a dramatic technique which reveals the character's inner thoughts and feelings.

Assonance: same vowel sounds repeating, e.g. 'Oh no, won't Joe go?'

Bathos: abrupt change from sublime to ridiculous for humorous effect.

Blank verse: lines of unrhymed iambic pentameter.

Compressed time: when the narrative is fast-forwarding through the action.

Descending tricolon: sentence with three parts, each decreasing in power, e.g. 'shouting, talking, whispering'.

Denouement: tying up loose ends, the resolution.

Diction: choice of words or vocabulary.

Didactic: used to describe literature designed to inform, instruct or pass on a moral message.

Dilated time: opposite compressed time, here the narrative is in slow motion.

Direct address: second person narrative, predominantly using the personal pronoun 'you'.

Dramatic action verb: manifests itself in physical action, e.g. I punched him in the face.

Dramatic irony: audience knows something that the character is unaware of.

Ellipsis: leaving out part of the story and allowing the reader to fill in the narrative gap.

End-stopped lines: poetic lines that end with punctuation.

Epistolary: letter or correspondence-driven narrative.

Flashback/Analepsis: going back in time to the past, interrupting the chronological sequence.

Flashforward/Prolepsis: going forward in time to the future, interrupting the chronological sequence.

Foreshadowing/Adumbrating: suggestion of plot developments that will occur later in the narrative.

Gothic: another strand of Romanticism, typically with a wild setting, a sensitive heroine, an older man with a 'piercing gaze', discontinuous structure, doppelgangers, guilt and the 'unspeakable' (according to Eve Kosofsky Sedgwick).

Hamartia: character flaw, leading to that character's downfall.

Hyperbole: exaggeration for effect.

Iambic pentameter: a line of ten syllables beginning with a lighter stress alternating with a heavier stress in its perfect form, which sounds like a heartbeat. The stress falls on the even syllables, numbers: 2, 4, 6, 8 and 10, e.g. 'When now I think you can behold such sights'.

Intertextuality: links to other literary texts.

Irony: amusing or cruel reversal of expected outcome or words meaning the opposite to their literal meaning.

Metafiction/Romantic irony: self-conscious exposure of the devices used to create 'the truth' within a work of fiction.

Motif: recurring image use of language or idea that connects the narrative together and creates a theme or mood, e.g. 'green light' in *The Great Gatsby*.

Oxymoron: contradictory terms combined, e.g. deafening silence.

Pastiche: imitation of another's work.

Pathetic fallacy: a form of personification whereby inanimate objects show human attributes, e.g. 'the sea smiled benignly'. The originator of the term, John Ruskin in 1856, used 'the cruel, crawling foam', from Kingsley's

The Sands of Dee, as an example to clarify what he meant by the 'morbid' nature of pathetic fallacy.

Personification: concrete or abstract object made human, often simply achieved by using a capital letter or a personal pronoun, e.g. 'Nature', or describing a ship as 'she'.

Pun/Double entendre: a word with a double meaning, usually employed in witty wordplay but not always.

Retrospective: account of events after they have occurred.

Romanticism: genre celebrating the power of imagination, spriritualism and nature.

Semantic/lexical field: related words about a single concept, e.g. king, queen and prince are all concerned with royalty.

Soliloquy: character thinks aloud, but is not heard by other characters (unlike in a monologue) giving the audience access to inner thoughts and feelings.

Style: choice of language, form and structure, and effects produced.

Synecdoche: one part of something referring to the whole, e.g. Carker's teeth represent him in *Dombey and Son*.

Syntax: the way words and sentences are placed together.

Tetracolon climax: sentence with four parts, culminating with the last part, e.g. 'I have nothing to offer but blood, toil, tears, and sweat ' (Winston Churchill).

ABOUT THE AUTHOR

Joe Broadfoot is a secondary school teacher of English and a soccer journalist, who also writes fiction and literary criticism. His former experiences as a DJ took him to far-flung places such as Tokyo, Kobe, Beijing, Hong

Kong, Jakarta, Cairo, Dubai, Cannes, Oslo, Bergen and Bodo. He is now PGCE and CELTA-qualified with QTS, a first-class honours degree in Literature and an MA in Victorian Studies (majoring in Charles Dickens). Drama is close to his heart as he acted in 'Macbeth' and 'A Midsummer Night's Dream' at the Royal Northern College of Music in Manchester. More recently, he has been teaching 'Much Ado About Nothing' to 'A' Level students at a secondary school in Buckinghamshire, 'An Inspector Calls' at a school in west London 'Heroes' at a school in Kent and 'A Christmas Carol' at a school in south London.

29344787R00039

Printed in Great Britain
by Amazon